DATE DUE

Everything You Need to Know About

Dealing with Sexual Assault

Sexual assault is a crime that can happen to anyone and leave the victim feeling lonely and depressed.

Everything You Need to Know About

Dealing with Sexual Assault

Laura Kaminker

The Rosen Publishing Group, Inc.
New York

This book is dedicated to all survivors of violence.

Published in 1998, 2000 by The Rosen Publishing Group, Inc.
29 East 21st Street, New York, NY 10010

Copyright © 1998, 2000 by The Rosen Publishing Group, Inc.

Revised Edition   OCLC 45442677

Library of Congress Cataloging-in-Publication Data

Kaminker, Laura.
    Everything you need to know about dealing with sexual assault / Laura Kaminker.
    p. cm—(The need to know library)
    Includes bibliographical references and index.
    Summary: Discusses the myths and facts surrounding sexual assault and rape, the physical and psychological consequences, suggests ways to stay safe, and explains what to do if sexually assaulted.
    ISBN: 0-8239-3303-2
    1. Rape—United States—juvenile literature. 2. Acquaintance rape—United States—juvenile literature. 3. Young women—Crimes against—United States—juvenile literature. [1. Rape. 2. Acquaintance rape. 3. Young women—Crimes against. 4. Dating violence.] 1. Title. 2. Series.
    HV656.1K35 1998 364.15'32—dc21

                                          98-7048
                                            CIP
                                               AC

Manufactured in the United States of America

Contents

Introduction: A Physical and Emotional Pain

I never thought it would happen to me. He was a perfect gentleman until last night. I thought I knew him.

He got only six months in jail. I have to live with the memory of what he did to me for the rest of my life.

It started when I was six and went on until I was twelve. I have no words to describe how I feel. All I know is secrecy, pain, guilt, and rage.

Sexual assault is an attack involving unwanted sexual contact between a victim and an assailant. Thousands of incidents of sexual assault are reported each year. Here are some alarming numbers from the Department of Justice's Bureau of Justice Statistics:

◆There were 330,000 victims of rape or sexual assault in the United States in 1998.

◆In over 70 percent of the rapes and sexual assaults committed, the victim knew the attacker.

◆Females age twelve or older were victims of rape or sexual assault at a rate fourteen times that of males.

◆Teenagers between the ages of sixteen and nineteen were most likely to be victims of rape and sexual assault.

◆Twelve- to fifteen-year-olds were raped or sexually assaulted at four times the rate of persons age fifty or older.

According to the Rape, Abuse and Incest National Network (RAINN), an organization devoted to helping survivors of rape and sexual assault, 28 percent of victims were raped by husbands and boyfriends, 35 percent by acquaintances, and 5 percent by other relatives.

Sexual assault can be a terrifying secret. Many rapes go unreported, thus allowing the rapist to go free. Why? Some victims feel ashamed and consider the assault a personal matter. They may also fear revenge from the attacker.

As you mature, society teaches you many myths and stereotypes about how men and women are supposed to

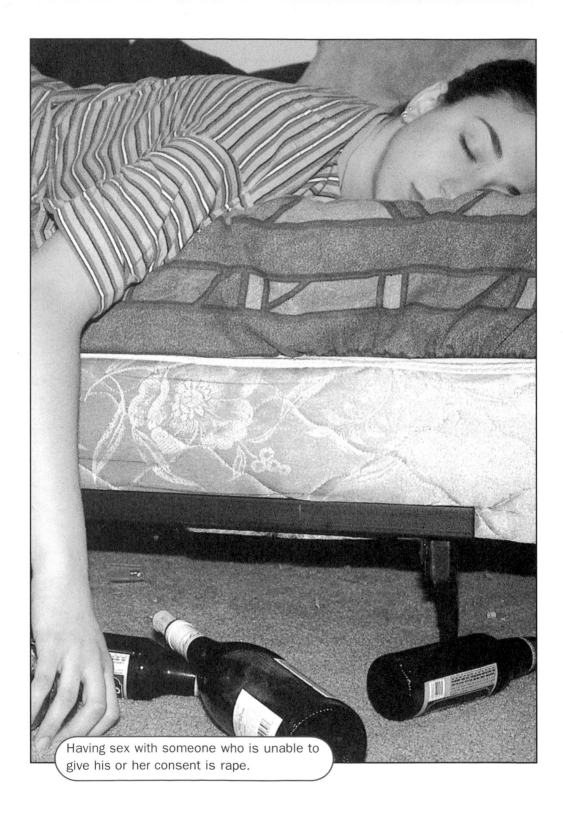

Having sex with someone who is unable to give his or her consent is rape.

Chapter One | What Is Sexual Assault?

*H*e locked the door and stood in front of it. He then grabbed my arm and pushed me over to the bed. I begged him to stop, but he refused. One hand was pressed over my mouth and his other hand was reaching under my clothes touching my body. Then he pulled down his pants and got into bed with me.

I was so frightened I wanted to scream, but nothing came out.

If someone makes you engage in any type of sexual activity against your will, it is sexual assault even if sexual intercourse does not occur. If someone forces you to have sex without your consent, it is rape. Rape is only one kind of sexual assault.

Rape and sexual assault are always violent crimes whether or not a weapon is used, and whether or not the victim is beaten in addition to being raped. Anyone who is sexually assaulted is hurt physically and emotionally—whether or not it shows on the outside.

Every person has the right to control his or her own body. No one has a right to touch your body without your permission. There are no exceptions to this rule. It does not matter how long you have known a person or if you have had sex with that person (or any other person) before. If two people are married, it does not mean that either person is entitled to sex if the other is against the idea. Any time someone is unwillingly forced to have sex, that person is being raped.

A person who is unable to give his or her consent to sexual activity has not said yes. If someone passes out from too much alcohol and another person has sex with him or her, that person has been raped. If a girl or boy is disabled and cannot understand what sex is, or resist unwanted sexual interactions, and someone makes him or her perform a sexual activity, it is sexual assault—a criminal offense.

The act of having sexual intercourse with someone under the legal age of consent is called statutory rape. The legal age is usually between fourteen and eighteen, depending on the state. If you are caught committing statutory rape, you will be arrested.

Sexual assault has nothing to do with how attractive

a man or a woman is. It has nothing to do with desire or passion. Rape and sexual assault come from a need for power and control. In rape, sex is a weapon. It is used to overpower, humiliate, and inflict pain on another person.

Rape does not discriminate. It happens to girls, women, boys, and men. It happens to straight and gay people. It happens to young kids and old people. It does not matter what a person wears, where he or she hangs out, or with whom he or she has sex. Rape is never the victim's fault.

Chapter Two

Separating Fact and Myth About Rape

W_ait a minute! He's so good looking. He wouldn't need to do something like that._

I'm not surprised that it happened. You wouldn't be either if you'd seen the way she acted around guys.

She dresses as if she wants to get raped. What are men supposed to think?

Although rape is very common, it is misunderstood. Many people's ideas about rape are really based on myths. A myth is a story that most people in society believe but that is not necessarily true. Some myths are harmless and fun. Other myths cause people pain and misinform our society of the truth. Let us look at some myths about sexual assault.

You can't figure out who is a rapist just by looking at people.

Who Is a Rapist?

When you hear the word rapist, what do you imagine? Do you picture a man with a gun who drags his victim into a dark alley? That is one stereotype of a rapist. It is what we are likely to see in the movies and on television. In reality, there is no such thing as "looking like a rapist." Rapists can come from all ethnic backgrounds and walks of life.

Who Can Be Raped?

Anyone—regardless of gender, age, or race—can be sexually assaulted. Sexual assault has nothing to do with a victim's looks, what he or she wears, where he or she hangs out, or what sexual experiences he or she may have had. Rape, like any other crime, is caused by the assailant. The victim is not responsible for what the assailant has done.

Acquaintance Rape and Date Rape: When It's Someone You Know

Acquaintance rape and date rape are the most commonly occurring examples of sexual assault. They are similar in that the victim is coerced or pressured into having unwanted sex with someone he or she knows. In a 1998 study by the Bureau of Justice Statistics, 74 percent of rape and sexual assault victims knew their assailants.

Acquaintance Rape

Acquaintance rape means that the victim knew his or her rapist. Unlike stranger rape—where the assailant usually picks his victim at random—assailants in acquaintance rape intend to assault a specific victim who they may know intimately. Date rape is an example of acquaintance rape. However, acquaintance rape may also include a relationship such as the one between:

- An employer and an employee
- A doctor and a patient
- A family friend and a young person

16

◆ A teacher and a student

◆ A husband and a wife

Acquaintance rape is becoming more and more common, particularly in schools and colleges where drugs and alcohol are easily accessible. These substances are used by assailants to impair the victim's ability to make healthy choices. On college campuses, the drug Rohypnol —often referred to as a "roofy"—is being used to render women unconscious so that they have no memory of what happened to them.

Date Rape

Date rape occurs when there is forced sexual intercourse between two people who are on a date. For example, you might have met the person at a party. Or maybe you have been dating the person for some time. Perhaps you have been talking to or even flirting with someone and he misunderstood your friendliness as an invitation for sex.

If a guy invites a girl to a movie or dinner, he does not have the right to expect sex in return, even if he pays for the movie or dinner. A person always has the right to choose whether or not he or she will have sex. Sex must always be between two consenting people.

Don't Be Misled: Rape Is Rape

Nobody has the right to make decisions for you. Sex without consent is rape. Saying "no" or "stop" is enough to let

Sexual assault does not change a person's sexual orientation. This is a common myth.

someone know that you don't want to have sex. The use of force or substances to make someone have sex is rape.

Rape and Sexual Orientation

Some people believe that a heterosexual man who is sexually assaulted by another man will become gay. Some people think that after a woman is raped, she will become a lesbian.

Rape has nothing to do with a person's sexual orientation and does not change someone's sexual orientation. Guys are not assaulted because they seem gay. Rape does not turn heterosexual women into lesbians.

The following pages are filled with some common myths and the facts about rape and sexual assault.

MYTHS	FACTS
Most rapists attack women they do not know in a park or on a deserted street.	The majority of victims know their assailants.
Rapists are men who are desperate for sex. If they had sex more often, they would not rape.	Rape has nothing to do with wanting or needing sex. Rape is a crime of violence and power.
No one can really be forced to have sex, except with a weapon. If the victim did not fight back, it wasn't rape.	A person can be overpowered without a weapon. It can be too dangerous or impossible to fight back.
Rape is violent only if the victim is beaten up, stabbed, or shot.	Rape is always a violent crime. Sexual assault of any kind inflicts violence on the victim's body, mind, and spirit.
You can tell if a person is a rapist by looking at him.	Appearances cannot predict who will commit rape. People from all walks of life commit sexual assault.
There is no such thing as date rape. Girls who have sex feel guilty later, so they say they were raped.	Many sexual assaults occur on dates, at parties, in schools, or in other social settings.
Rape is something you never get over. A victim of rape will never have a normal life again.	Though rape is devastating, it is possible to recover fully. Many survivors go on to lead successful, fulfilling lives.

MYTHS	FACTS
Most rapists are African-American men, and their victims are white women.	Both victims and assailants come from all backgrounds. In the majority of sexual assaults, the victim is the same race as the assailant.
Good-looking guys who can get a lot of sex do not rape.	How often a man has sex has nothing to do with sexual assault. Rape is not caused by the need for sex, but a need to assert power.
Only young, attractive women are raped.	Anyone can be raped. Rape is not an expression of sexual desire, so appearances do not matter.
Only gay guys are sexually assaulted.	Homosexual and heterosexual men can be sexually assaulted. Rape has nothing to do with sexual orientation.
If a woman is raped, it is her own fault.	Rape is a crime. Like any crime, it is the criminal who causes it, not the victim.

MYTHS	FACTS
A woman who wears sexy clothes, stays out late, or has sex with many different men is asking for trouble. If she gets raped, she has no one to blame but herself.	You may think a woman's behavior is wrong, but it is her right to control her own body. No one has a right to touch a woman's body without her consent.
Boys are very rarely sexually assaulted.	Boys under the age of ten are victims of sexual assault almost as frequently as girls of that age. Teenage boys are also frequently sexually assaulted.
Women who are raped become lesbians.	Rape does not change a person's sexual orientation.
Once a girl sleeps with a guy, she can never say no to him. He is allowed to force her to have sex because she said yes before.	Everyone has the right to say no. No one is ever obligated to have sex—no matter what his or her previous sexual relationship was with the person.
If a guy spends a lot of money on a girl, he has a right to have sex with her.	No one ever has a right to anyone else's body.

A survivor of rape may feel frightened or threatened in certain situations, but over time, these feelings of fear will pass.

Chapter Three

The Consequences

I *hated myself after the assault. I felt ashamed and embarrassed. Now I don't want to go out for fear that people will see me and know what happened.*

He works at a clothing store near my house. I go out of my way to avoid him. Just seeing him again after what he did to me makes me so angry. It's as if he's allowed to have a normal life and I can't. I don't know what to do or think anymore.

Sexual assault is a traumatic event. It causes physical and emotional pain that lasts a very long time. Since each person is unique, every victim of sexual assault will have a different reaction. There is no right way to react to sexual assault. Certain reactions, however, are common.

Short-Term Consequences

A person who has been sexually assaulted is terrified and confused. The victim may be bruised, bleeding, or aching all over. A woman may be worried that she is pregnant. There may be concern about contracting HIV or other sexually transmitted diseases. If there are no outward signs of the assault, such as bruises, the victim may worry that people will not believe him or her.

A male victim experiences the same fear and confusion as a female victim. He feels ashamed and isolated. He may be physically hurt, but he may be too embarrassed to go see a doctor.

Most survivors have trouble sleeping in the days and weeks after the assault. The person may have nightmares and feel extremely frightened and jumpy. A survivor might have no energy and feel unable to move.

During this time, many sexual assault survivors say they feel as if they are losing their minds. This can last for days, weeks, or months, depending on the person and what happened. That is why talking about the experience helps the healing process begin.

Long-Term Consequences

Full recovery from rape or sexual assault takes a long time. Nightmares and terrifying flashbacks can continue off and on for years. Survivors may often feel unsafe, fearful, and anxious. Other long-term effects of sexual

Sexual assault is a very traumatic experience. It takes time, as well as love and support, to heal.

assault vary depending on the circumstances of the assault. For example, a girl who was raped in her own home may be afraid of being home alone. A girl who was raped on a date may be afraid of dating.

Many survivors of sexual assault suffer from depression. They may feel sad, hopeless, and lonely. They may think about suicide. Not every survivor has these feelings, but they are not unusual.

Acquaintance Rape and Date Rape: The Painful Truth

Maria thought she knew her date, Jason—until he sexually assaulted her. After the attack, she began to realize that Jason had been controlling and obsessive. He was always critical of every little thing she did, and he never listened to her opinions.

Rape by someone you know is no less terrible than stranger rape. In addition to the emotional and physical consequences of having been raped, the victim also has to deal with feelings of betrayal. The closer the person was to the victim, the stronger those feelings of betrayal are likely to be.

Many cases of date or acquaintance rape are not reported because the victim fears no one will believe him or her. He or she probably feels in some way responsible for the assault or may think it was not really rape. When

Date rape can be particularly awful, especially if the survivor is unwilling to report the crime and has to see the assailant at school.

reporting a rape or sexual assault, the victim will be asked a lot of questions that may be humiliating and painful to answer. The stigma of shame is the main reason why most incidents of sexual assault go unreported.

Fifteen-year-old Samantha was afraid to tell anyone that Mitchell, a college senior, sexually assaulted her. Mitchell was the son of a close friend of the family. She felt no one would believe her. "Everyone sees Mitchell as the nice guy," Samantha said to herself. "But he raped me."

Victims of rape undergo not only physical issues but also emotional ones, such as betrayal, fear, confusion, guilt, and self-hatred. It is important to report a sexual assault and to get all the medical attention that you need. By reporting the crime, you will not only receive vital medical and emotional help but you may also be preventing someone else from experiencing the same trauma.

The Littlest Victims: Sexual Abuse and Children

Sexual assault at any age is emotionally and physically damaging, but for very young people it is especially traumatic.

In a 1997 report, the Bureau of Justice Statistics offered these numbers on sexual abuse:

- ◆ About 80 percent of rape victims were under the age of thirty. Victims younger than twelve accounted for 15 percent of those raped, and another 29 percent of rape victims were between twelve and seventeen.

- ◆ Ninety percent of the victims age twelve years and younger knew their assailant. Family members victimized 43 percent of these young victims.

Unlike assault, which may be a one-time occurrence, sexual abuse is a pattern of behavior against the victim. The abuse often happens many times—even for years—so that the young person is constantly living in fear. Children who are abused by a family member (an act

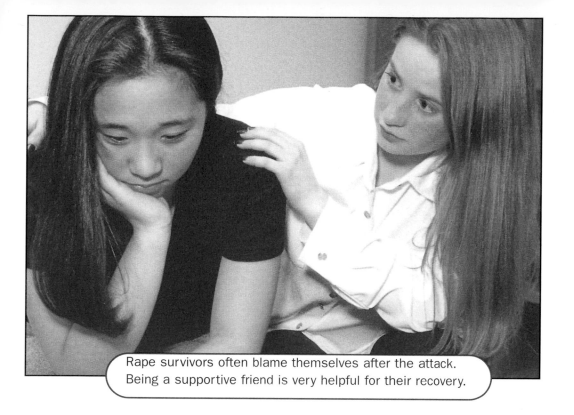

Rape survivors often blame themselves after the attack. Being a supportive friend is very helpful for their recovery.

called incest) or other adults are usually silenced with guilt, intimidation, and violence. For this reason, victims of childhood sexual abuse often don't tell anyone about it. Some common lies told to children to silence them are:

If you tell your mom about our secret, you will be hurting her.

If you tell anyone about this, you will break up the family.

Who are they going to believe anyway, a kid or a grown-up?

Many survivors of sexual abuse suffer emotional difficulties. Victims often become depressed, develop eating disorders, abuse drugs, have difficulty with intimate relationships, or become suicidal. Most survivors do not realize that others have been through a similar ordeal, which may leave them feeling desperately alone.

As a child, it can be difficult to know that what someone is doing to you is wrong, especially if that person is a trusted adult or family member. But no one has the right to touch or hurt you in a way that makes you feel uncomfortable. That is why it is important to tell someone and get yourself the help you need to end the abuse.

If someone is sexually abusing you or someone you know, you must tell someone you trust, immediately. If you are afraid to tell a family member, then tell your teacher, your religious adviser, or even the police.

Self–Blame: A Common Reaction

If only I hadn't let him into my room . . .

I should have been able to fight him off . . .

The most common reaction to sexual assault is self-blame. But all rape survivors need to know that they are not to blame. The rapist is responsible for the assault, not the victim.

So why do victims blame themselves? Rape temporarily destroys a person's sense of safety and control. A normal experience such as dating, jogging, or staying home is suddenly transformed into a nightmare. The

Telling your parents about sexual assault can be a good first step in your healing.

rapist had complete control over the victim, which is very painful to accept. The victim does not want to think about this, so she searches for a more comforting explanation. In a way, it is easier to think "I must have done something wrong" than to think "This person had complete control over me, and I was totally helpless."

How many of us have heard about a rape and said something like "She shouldn't have gone out at night"? Thinking about rape frightens us. If rape can happen to anyone, it can happen to us. So we tell ourselves that her going out at night was what caused the rape. Saying something like "I won't do that, so I won't be raped" makes us feel less vulnerable. Everyone has heard remarks like these, including the rape survivor.

So it is natural that a victim would think "What did I do to cause this?" or "How could I have prevented it?" Also, many survivors are confused by the myths about rape. If you believe that girls who are raped must have "asked for it," and then you yourself are assaulted, what will you think? You can see how much damage these myths can cause.

Fantasy Is Not Reality

Sometimes sexual assault victims blame their secret thoughts. Some girls may fantasize about certain sexual acts that they might not want to do in real life. These thoughts cannot lead to rape. Many young men feel attracted to other men and wonder what it would be like to be physical with another guy. These thoughts are common, and there is no harm in them. If a guy had these fantasies, and then a man sexually assaulted him, he might think he had sent a signal to that man. But again, these thoughts cannot lead to rape. It is natural and normal to have sexual fantasies. They cannot hurt us.

Reactions from Others

But most of the time, unfortunately, family and friends are not always understanding and supportive. Parents may find the situation too upsetting to deal with, so they pretend nothing happened. Perhaps they do not realize what an enormous and horrible experience the rape was. Or they do not know what to do.

Sometimes boyfriends, friends, and family members may question the survivor's choices or judgment. They may not want to hear about the experience. In an effort to be comforting, they may say insensitive things.

If you are a survivor of sexual assault, try to share your feelings with someone who believes and understands you. Remember, you did not do anything wrong, no matter what anyone else thinks or says.

Chapter Four

Recovery

I took me a long time to get over being raped, much longer than I had imagined. Today I can talk about it and it's okay. I don't feel ashamed or embarrassed anymore.

No one recovers from a trauma all at once. Recovery from sexual assault is a gradual process, and not always a steady one. There will be some good days and some bad days.

Stages of Recovery

Psychologists have found that there are five stages of recovery.

- **Denial**. The victim pretends the assault did not happen. She may be ashamed or terrified of what other people will say. She may be in shock and not understand what has happened.

- **Self-blame**. Next, victims blame themselves, thinking "If only I hadn't . . ."

- **Victimization**. In the third stage, the survivor understands that she did not cause the attack and that she truly was a victim. This is a very painful and difficult time. At this point, a survivor feels depressed and hopeless, and wonders how she will go on.

- **Survival**. Eventually, the victim makes a decision that she will get on with her life. She understands that the assault was a horrible event but that it does not have to ruin her life. She decides to move beyond it.

- **Recovery** This is when the survivor learns and takes action. She knows that the assault happened and that she has survived. She decides to learn from the experience in any way she can. This can be a period of tremendous inner growth during which survivors use their new knowledge and strength to help others.

These stages are a general description, not a rule. One person may be in denial for a few hours or for years after the assault. Many factors can affect a person's recovery, including how much support the survivor gets and her own self-esteem. Everyone can recover from sexual assault. Rape is horrible, but you do not have to let it destroy your life.

Recovery and Sex

After a sexual assault, many survivors lose interest in sex for a while. A woman with a steady sexual partner may just want to cuddle and kiss but not be sexually active. When she starts dating again, she may not want to get involved physically. These are natural, normal feelings, and they pass with time. Some survivors of sexual assault want to have sex soon afterward. As one woman put it: "I needed to reassure myself that that part of my life had not been stolen from me." Again, each individual recovers in his or her own way.

Don't Keep It Inside

The key to recovering from a trauma such as sexual assault is to talk about it. When we talk about our experience and our feelings, we release our pain. It becomes easier to bear. If we do not talk about it, the pain stays inside us and can come out in other ways. This can lead to problems such as depression, drug abuse, and eating disorders. A person who is depressed may not realize that a past sexual assault is the root of the problem. She may think: "That happened so long ago, how could it make me depressed today?" Only when she begins to talk about what happened does she start feeling better.

Chapter Five

What If It Happens to Me or to Someone I Love?

If you have been raped or sexually assaulted, or if you were assaulted in the past, tell someone. Find the person you love and trust the most and tell him or her. Remember, you did not do anything wrong. You do not have to carry the burden alone. You need comfort and support. Reach out to someone as soon as you can.

Get Medical Care

After a sexual assault, it is very important to see a doctor. Pregnancy, sexually transmitted diseases (STDs), and injuries are all easier to deal with if they are discovered early. Many conditions are easy to treat in an early stage but can cause major problems if left untreated. It may frighten you to consider this possibility, but it must be addressed. If you have confided in a friend or family member, ask him or her to go to the doctor with you. Having someone there with you will make it easier.

Even if you choose not to tell anyone about the assault, you still need to take care of yourself. Maybe you know a doctor or a clinic that you or a friend has visited. If there is a Planned Parenthood in your town, call them for an appointment. Planned Parenthood treats men, too. Many hospitals have walk-in clinics. If you are not sure where to go, look in the yellow pages under "Women's Health Care" or "Medical Care, Low Cost" or "Victims' Services."

If you go to a doctor immediately after the assault, do not bathe or wash before you go. The doctor or nurse will take samples of bodily fluids and hair, which can be used as evidence if you decide to report the crime to the police. (You do not have to make that decision while you are in the hospital.) If a certain amount of time has passed since the assault, the hospital will not be able to collect evidence.

The confidentiality of medical care varies from state to state. If you are concerned that your parents or a child protection agency will be informed about your assault or abuse, call the Rape, Abuse and Incest National Network (RAINN) hotline at (800) 656-HOPE or Childhelp USA at (800) 4-A-CHILD to find out about the laws in your state.

At the Hospital: Your Health

If you go to a hospital or medical center, tell the person at the desk that you were sexually assaulted. You will be taken to a private area and seen immediately by a nurse or doctor. He or she will ask you questions about the attack. You may be embarrassed to answer them, but it is important to be honest so that you can be treated properly. The doctor is there to help you, not to judge you.

First you will be treated for any injury that requires immediate attention. Then you will be brought to a private examining room. It is necessary to have a pelvic exam, similar to the one given at a gynecologist's office. This is done by a female doctor or nurse. A counselor, social worker, or volunteer may also be there to offer comfort and support.

To a person who has just been sexually assaulted, a pelvic exam can feel like even more intrusion and humiliation. Though it will not be a pleasant experience, the doctor will try to be as gentle and respectful as possible. She will explain each step of the procedure before it happens.

The doctor or nurse will write notes about your condition. She will give you two injections of antibiotics to help protect you against sexually transmitted diseases. She will also ask you if you use any method of birth control. If you were not using birth control at the time of the assault, she may offer you a morning-after pill to

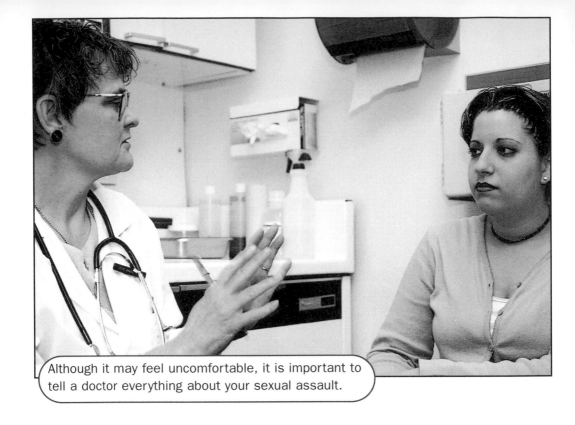

Although it may feel uncomfortable, it is important to tell a doctor everything about your sexual assault.

prevent pregnancy. If the hospital does not use morning-after pills, the doctor can tell you where you can get one.

The doctor or nurse will give you a pregnancy test and tests for sexually transmitted diseases. She will also tell you to have the tests taken again in two weeks. This is very important. Sexually transmitted diseases may not appear until two weeks after an assault.

Male victims of sexual assault also need medical attention. For a man, the hospital procedure will be the same, except for the pelvic exam. It is just as important for men to be checked and treated for sexually trans-mitted diseases and to have a follow-up exam two weeks later.

At the Hospital: Your Rights

Some hospitals automatically contact the police in all cases of sexual assault. This does not mean that you have to make a police report. Only you can decide whether or not to report the assault to the police. If you do not want to report at that time, you can change your mind and go to the police later. Your medical records will be used as evidence.

Most hospital personnel are trained to deal with victims of sexual assault. While it is unlikely that a doctor or nurse will be insensitive or disrespectful, it could (and occasionally does) happen. If you have an unpleasant experience with a doctor or nurse, report the incident to the hospital, to your local victims' services agency, or to the police. It is also your right to speak to a lawyer if you feel your civil rights have been violated.

You have an obligation to yourself to get proper medical attention. If you feel you have not received it, ask for a new doctor or go somewhere else.

Emotional First Aid

Just as you need to take care of yourself physically, you need to take care of yourself emotionally, too. One way to do that is to speak to a rape crisis counselor. You can do this by calling a rape crisis center in your area. Many hospitals have free counseling and support groups for survivors of rape and sexual assault. If you go to an

41

adolescent health center, you can talk to a sexual assault counselor. Counseling is completely confidential. Your counselor will not tell anyone else what you say.

A counselor can never take the place of your friends and family. However, no matter how understanding your friends and family are, they may not have any experience in dealing with sexual assault. Survivors of all ages have found that talking to a counselor or therapist gave them relief.

No matter how long ago it happened, no matter what the circumstances were, a rape counselor will understand. The counselor will never blame you and never judge you. Remember: It is never too late to talk about the rape. Talking about it begins the healing process.

To Report or Not to Report?

Sexual assault is a crime. A person who rapes or sexually assaults someone has committed a criminal act.

Many victims of sexual assault, however, do not report the crime to the police. Some people are afraid that the police will not believe them or will treat them badly. Some victims are afraid that if they report the crime, it will become public. Others do not want to admit that the assault actually happened.

The decision of whether or not to report an assault is a personal one. Here are some things to think about:

◆ Some people find that reporting the rape makes

them feel stronger and more in control of their lives. It is a way of saying "I won't let him get away with this."

◆ Most police officers now receive special training in handling sexual assault cases. Although no one can guarantee how an individual police officer will act, most will treat a person reporting rape in a respectful, sympathetic manner.

◆ Sexual assault, like any other crime, can be reported long after the event. It is best if a rape is reported right away, but it is not necessary.

◆ You have the right to have a friend or counselor present when you speak to the police.

If you are deciding whether or not to go to the police, you may want to discuss the issues with a counselor.

My Best Friend Was Raped. How Can I Help Her?

If you have a friend who was sexually assaulted, she needs to know that she is not alone and that you are there for her. If she wants to talk about what happened, listen. Avoid saying "I know how you feel," since no one really knows how anyone else feels, especially if they have not gone through the trauma themselves. Instead try saying "I'm so glad you're okay." Tell her you care about her and want to help. Do not be afraid to listen and not say anything. Just be there for her.

And please, be careful. She needs your unconditional support and not questions like "Why did you go out with him?" or "Why did you let him come back to your room?" She may think you are blaming her—even if you aren't.

If you are the first person she has told about the assault, your reaction is very important. If she gets love and support from you, she is on her way to healing. But if she feels judged and blamed, her pain will increase and last longer.

Another great thing you can do for your friend is recommend counseling. However, do not make an appointment for her or take her to a counselor. Do not ever try to force her to see a therapist.

When a friend is hurting, it is natural to want to take care of her. But remember that a survivor of sexual assault has temporarily lost control of her body and her life. Recovery is the process of regaining that control. In order for that to happen, survivors need to make their own decisions and take care of themselves. Just listen to her, believe her, and be there for her. Do not try to do everything for her.

Everyone heals in his or her own way. Your friend cannot open up until he or she is ready. For some people, it may be an hour after the assault. For others, it may be years.

Sometimes my daughter seems depressed and withdrawn. I think, "Could this still be from the rape?" It has been so long. I want to help her, but I'm not sure how.

Friends and family are often supportive immediately after an assault. But once the survivor is out of the crisis stage—when the person looks fine, and things seem to be back to normal—friends and family may assume the problem is over. People usually do not feel comfortable talking about rape in the first place, so when they see a survivor acting normally, they want to believe everything is all right. Let the person know that she can come to you at any time and you will be there to listen.

Sometimes people think they should not mention the rape because it will upset the victim more. This can make the survivor feel isolated and alone. If someone you care about was sexually assaulted, do not pretend it did not happen. She is thinking about it whether she says anything or not. Ask her how she is doing and if she wants to talk about it.

If your friend was raped, you may first think about who did it. You are probably angry and want the assailant to be punished for his crime. While it is natural to feel this way, it does not help the survivor. Try to focus on her needs first.

You may want to talk to a counselor about how you feel. Sexual assault affects not only the victim but also the victim's family and friends.

Let your friend know that you are there to listen. Just knowing that you are there to support her can be a tremendous help.

Chapter Six

Staying Safe

Unfortunately, there is no way to make us completely safe from sexual assault. But using common sense can make us safer.

- ◆ If you live in an apartment, there should be a gate on any window that opens onto a fire escape or street. Always keep your door locked when you are home and when you are out. Never let anyone in unless you know who it is.

- ◆ You deserve safety. If your apartment building does not have a good lock on the front door, or if the entrance is dark, speak to your landlord. Get your neighbors to back you up. If the landlord does not listen, tell him you will complain to the town or city. Make sure you follow up on this.

- When you walk home or to your car, take a well-traveled route and have your keys where you can easily get to them. At night, walk with a friend. If you jog or ride a bike, avoid deserted areas and go with a friend. There is safety in numbers.

- If you go shopping at night, park close to the store to avoid a long walk through an empty parking lot.

- Do not hitchhike. Many teenagers have been raped and killed while hitchhiking. There is just no way to know who will give you a safe ride. The same goes for picking up hitchhikers. You would not let a total stranger into your home, so do not invite one into your car.

Be Assertive!

Often, girls are more inclined than guys to want to please people and be liked. Some guys will take advantage of that and try to pressure them into having sex. But girls who know what they want and assert themselves are more likely to be respected. Do not let a guy force you to have sex with him just because he wants you to.

If you really love me, you'll sleep with me. You got me all excited. You can't stop now.

If you won't have sex with me, I'll find some-one who will.

A guy who pressures you about sex is thinking only of himself. You should be thinking of yourself. Any guy who does not respect your choices doesn't deserve you.

Sexual assault, including date rape, is not completely preventable because you cannot control what the other person does. There are some other things, however, you can control. For example, learning how to take control of a situation will make you more confident in all areas of your life. The more you assert yourself, the better you will feel—and the safer you will be.

Taking Action

Here are some suggestions to help reduce your chances of being sexually assaulted:

- When going out on a date with someone new, always let your parents or someone responsible know where you will be.

- Take note of the person's body language. Is the person too possessive or controlling? Does he respect your opinions?

- Trust your instincts. If you feel that you are somewhere that is too deserted, suggest going to a place where there are more people.

Whenever you go out with someone new, let your parents know who you're going with, where you're going, and when you'll be back.

- If you feel a guy is putting pressure on you, tell him that you want him to stop. If he does not listen, you should leave.

- Avoid alcohol and drugs. Fifty-five percent of college-age women who reported sexual assaults said they had been drinking or using drugs.

Here are some things young people have done to make themselves safer:

Whenever I go out, I make sure I have money on me, just in case I need to get home on my own. It makes me feel safer and more independent.

I wanted to go to Michael's party. But all of his friends were going to be there, and I wouldn't know anybody. So I asked Deb and Mark to come along. I just felt more comfortable with them there.

The first time we went out, Jackson wanted to go to his house because his parents were away. Maybe it would have been fine, but why take a chance? I suggested we go to a movie instead. I didn't want to be alone with him right away.

Drugs and Alcohol

It is important to be careful about alcohol or any other drug, especially if you are with people you do not know. Drugs decrease our ability to judge if a situation is safe or not. If you are drunk or high, you might not realize that your date is coming on too strong or that you have wandered far away from the party. If you do drink alcohol, do so in moderation. And if you are with people you do not know, try to avoid alcohol entirely.

This does not mean that a woman who was drinking when she was assaulted caused her own rape. Her drinking did not make someone else abuse her. But if you are not drinking, you are more alert and more in control. Being clearheaded can help you avoid or stop an assault.

Just as important, do not stay with a guy who is drunk. If your date seems out of control, look for another way to get home. Just because you began the evening with a guy does not mean you have to stay with him—especially if he makes you feel uncomfortable or puts you in danger.

As we spoke about in chapter 2, there is a drug commonly used in date rapes called Rohypnol, or a "roofy." The drug is illegal in the United States. It is a powerful sedative that can last up to twelve hours. It can be slipped into drinks, and since it has no color, taste, or smell, you can swallow it and not know it. According to the Partnership for a Drug-Free America, Rohypnol creates a sleepy, relaxed, and drunk feeling. It can leave a person vulnerable to an assailant. Therefore, be aware of your surroundings. Whenever you are drinking with other people, you should always pour your own drink and keep a careful watch over it.

Not all guys are rapists. It is important to trust people, but trust has to be earned. Until it is, you should be careful.

Recognize Danger Signs

Studies have shown that a rapist's behavior often follows certain patterns. Although not all rapists fall into these categories, it is wise to watch out for and avoid these types of behavior:

• Invasion of your personal space

• A total lack of respect for your feelings

- Being constantly told that you are wrong
- Being reminded that he knows better than you do
- Hostile, controlling, and obsessive behavior
- Desensitization to and acceptance of violence

If you find yourself in a situation that feels danger-ous, try to draw attention to yourself. Do not go any-where alone with someone you do not know or feel comfortable with. Yell, scream, or bang on the wall—whatever it takes to be heard. Make enough noise so that someone will hear you. It is better to be embar-rassed than assaulted.

Self-Defense Is the Best Offense

Self-defense training is a very healthy thing to learn. It increases your strength and your self-confidence—and it is fun. One of the best things about self-defense is that size and strength do not matter. Women and men of all ages and abilities can learn how to defend them-selves. Many rape survivors find that learning self-defense helps them rebuild their self-confidence. People who know self-defense techniques are better equipped to handle a dangerous situation.

Some people believe that during a sexual assault, it is more dangerous to fight back. No one knows whether or not this is true. But many rapists threaten to kill their

Learning self-defense is a great way to boost your confidence and protect yourself against assault.

victims. Many survivors say that they believed it was a real possibility that their assailant would kill them.

Trust yourself. If you are assaulted, do whatever you have to do to get through the situation. If you can get away, go! If you think you know what you are doing, try to defend yourself. But if your assailant has a weapon, or if he is much bigger and stronger than you are, there may be no way to fight back.

Rape crisis counselors say this: "If you survived, you did the right thing." Not all rape victims survive. If you find yourself in a dangerous situation, trust your judgment. Do what you must to stay alive. As terrible as it is to be raped, nothing is more important than your life.

No Simple Solution

Unfortunately, there is no magic solution that will guarantee your safety. Even the most careful person can become a victim of sexual assault. It does not mean the victim was careless or just let it happen. It just means that the danger is very real, and he or she was unlucky.

Education = Prevention

Many of us are angry that we cannot jog in a park or go on a date without the fear of sexual violence. If you want things to change, get involved! Demand better security at your school or in your community. Volunteer at your local rape crisis center. Get involved with groups that are working to reduce the risks of rape and sexual assault.

We need to understand more about why certain men commit sexual assault and help them stop. In schools and youth centers, guys are joining groups to explore what it means to be a man and to help deal with the pressures of manhood. These groups are starting to redefine what it means to be a real man.

And most important, do not miss an opportunity to educate others about rape and sexual assault. How you speak about rape—and your reactions to what other people say—may be your best weapon of prevention.

You Own Your Body

In an ideal world there would be no violence and fear. Sexual assault would not even be an issue. But this world is not perfect. We must make choices and deal with the consequences of both our own actions and the actions of others.

Rape, sexual assault, and sexual abuse are sad and disturbing aspects of society. In every attack, the offender's actions drastically change the victim's life. It is the victim who is, in effect, punished for the crime of the attacker. The process of healing can be long and hard. Some circumstances are beyond our control. However, we can avoid these situations and learn how to deal with them if they do occur.

It is important for young men and women to empower themselves with self-respect and self-confidence. Asserting yourself is important. If you are the victim of a crime, you must not feel guilty or ashamed. Seek medical and emotional help. Do not allow sexual assault to destroy your life.

Glossary

acquaintance rape   Forced sexual intercourse or other sexual contact between two people who know each other.

confidential   When something spoken or written is kept secret.

consent   To give approval or permission.

date rape   Forced sexual intercourse or other sexual contact between a dating couple or while on a date.

depression   An illness that causes someone to feel sad for a long period of time.

eating disorder   A disease, such as anorexia nervosa or bulimia nervosa, that involves a person's eating habits, weight, body image, and self-esteem.

entitled   Having the right to do something.

evidence   Facts or proof that something happened.

flashback   An image of an earlier event that appears in a person's mind.

heterosexual   Having sexual interest in persons of the opposite sex.

HIV   The virus that causes AIDS.

homosexual Having sexual interest in persons of the same sex.

incest Sexual activity between family members.

morning-after pill A pill prescribed by doctors to terminate a pregnancy.

pelvic exam An internal exam given by a doctor to examine the vagina, the cervix, and the reproductive organs.

psychologist A person who studies the science of mind and behavior.

rape Forced sexual intercourse (or other sexual act) against the will of a victim.

sexual assault An attack involving unwanted sexual contact between a victim and an assailant.

sexually transmitted disease (STD) A disease that is spread by sexual activity.

statutory rape Sexual intercourse with a person who is under the legal age of consent (the age at which the law considers the person fully responsible for his or her actions).

stereotype An oversimplified opinion based on limited or false information.

trauma An event that causes physical injury and/or great mental or emotional stress.

victimization Behavior that makes someone a victim.

Where to Go for Help

If you have been raped, look in the front section of the white pages under "Sexual Assault Services" or "Victims' Services" to find a rape crisis center in your area. If you decide to report a rape, look in the front part of the white pages for a "Sex Crimes Report Line" or call your local police department and they will transfer your call. You can also reach the police by dialing 911 on any phone.

In the United States

Childhelp USA
(800) 4-A-CHILD (2-24453)

National Center for Victims of Crime
2111 Wilson Boulevard, Suite 300
Arlington, VA 22201
(800) FYI-CALL (394-2255)
Web site: http://www.ncvc.org

National Coalition Against Sexual Assault
125 North Enola Drive
Enola, PA 17025
(717) 728-9764
Web site: http://www.ncasa.org

Planned Parenthood
810 Seventh Avenue
New York, NY 10019
(800) 230-7526
Web site: http://www.plannedparenthood.org

The Rape, Abuse and Incest National Network
    (RAINN)
635-B Pennsylvania Avenue SE
Washington, DC 20003
(800) 656-HOPE
Web site: http://www.rainn.org

Sexual Assault Information Page
Web site:
    http://www.cs.utk.edu/~bartley/saInfoPage.html

Smart Date
P.O. Box 13232
San Luis Obispo, CA 93401
Web site: http://www.smartdate.com

In Canada

Fredericton Sexual Assault Crisis Centre
P.O. Box 174
Fredericton, NB E3B 4Y9
(506) 454-0437
Web site: http://www.discribe.ca/fsacc

Kids Help Phone
(800) 668-6868
Web site: http://kidshelp.sympatico.ca

Ottawa Rape Crisis Centre
P.O. Box 20206
Ottawa, ON K1N 9P4
(613) 562-2333
Web site: http://www.orcc.net

Vancouver Rape Relief and Women's Shelter
Web site: http://www.rapereliefshelter.bc.ca

Victoria Women's Sexual Assault Centre
754 Broughton Street
Victoria, BC V8W 1E1
(250) 383-3232
Web site: http://www.islandnet.com/~vwsac

For Further Reading

Bode, Janet. *The Voices of Rape*. Danbury, CT: Franklin Watts, 1998.

Loiselle, Mindy B., and Leslie B. Wright. *Back on Track: Boys Dealing with Sexual Abuse*. Brandon, VT: Safer Society Press, 1997.

McLaren, Karla. *Rebuilding the Garden: Healing the Spiritual Wounds of Childhood Sexual Assault*. Columbia, CA: Laughing Tree Press, 1997.

Parrot, Andrea. *Coping with Date Rape and Acquaintance Rape*. New York: Rosen Publishing Group, 1999.

Phillips, Louise. *Moving On: A Journey Through Sexual Assault*. Cincinnati, OH: Seven Hills Book Distributors, 1996.

Reinert, Dale R. *Sexual Abuse and Incest*. Springfield, NJ: Enslow Publishers, 1997.

Stoppard, Miriam. *Sex Ed: Growing Up, Relationships, and Sex*. New York: DK Publishing, Inc., 1998.

Williams, Mary E. *Date Rape* (At Issue). San Diego, CA: Greenhaven Press, 1998.

Index

About the Author

Laura Kaminker has worked as a rape crisis counselor, helped train emergency-room advocates, and gives workshops on sexual assault to schools and youth centers. She is the author of the award-winning video *Date Rape: Behind Closed Doors* and has written and spoken publicly about her own recovery from rape. She lives in New York City with her partner, Allan Wood, and their two dogs.

Acknowledgments

Thank you to the women of BWARE, whose support helped me end my silence. And thank you to everyone at Mount Sinai RCIP who help me to continue to speak out.

Photo Credits

Cover photo by Ira Fox; pp. 2, 22, 25, 46, 50, 54 by Les Mills; pp. 10, 15, 18, 27, 40 by Brian T. Silak; p. 8 by Ethan Zindler; pp. 29, 31 by John Bentham.